Songwriting for Sync

A Beginner's Q&A Guide to Writing for TV and Film

Three Kings Publishing

Songwriting for Sync: A Beginner's Q&A Guide to Writing for TV and Film

Copyright © 2022 by Corey Lee Barker

ISBN 978-1-947018-21-1

All rights reserved.

No part of this publication may be reproduced, stored in a retrieval system, or transmitted in any form or by any means, without prior permission in writing of the publisher, nor be otherwise circulated in any form of binding or cover other than which it is published and without a similar condition including this condition being imposed on the subsequent purchaser.

Three Kings Publishing
115 Canterbury Court
Princeton Kentucky 42445
threekingspublishing@gmail.com

A portion of every Three Kings book sale is given to support education through the nonprofit Future Hope Africa.

Songwriting for Sync

A Beginner's Q&A Guide to Writing for TV and Film

by Corey Lee Barker

Copyright © 2022 by Corey Lee Barker

SONGWRITING FOR SYNC

Beginner's Q&A Guide to Writing for TV and Film

ADVANCE PRAISE

"When Corey's name is on a song, you know you can expect to hear high-quality writing and production. Everything he sends me as a music supervisor is ready for placement in film/TV—and he makes my job easier because he is so business and music savvy."
—*Shantell Ogden, Award-winning Singer/Songwriter and Music Supervisor*

"Corey Lee Barker is one of the hardest-working, most gifted and talented songwriters in this town. I'm proud to call him a friend and congratulate him on all of his accomplishments and successes."
—*Buddy Jewell, Winner of* Nashville Star: Season 1

"Corey Lee Barker is one of the most in-depth, committed songwriters and visionaries I know. He's spent many hours here at MC1 Nashville writing and co-writing with hundreds of artists and songwriters. He's a perfectionist and can forevermore write a song."
—*Darlene Fowler, President of MC1 Nashville*

"How long does it take Corey Lee Barker to finish a lyri—OH MY GOD, HE'S DONE!"
—*David Norris, Producer, Norrisong Productions*

"Corey is not only an amazing songwriter who has touched many with his lyrics; to be able to read his books and continue to learn with him is priceless. When you read Corey's books, I can guarantee you will smile, laugh, and enjoy your own adventures in songwriting."
—*Jacqueline Burke and J.C. Veaudrey, Brandy Records Canada*

"Every single time I have requested a song from Corey for one of my artists, he always sends me a potential hit. I've been cutting Corey's songs for over twenty years, and there's not a nicer guy than Corey Barker."
—*Jim Cartwright, Fame & Fortune Entertainment and Records*

"Always good and helpful info. You can rely on Corey to get it straight; this is a major and overlooked part of songwriting."
—*Paul Castoe, President of the Tennessee Songwriters Association International*

"I don't know him. I just work here."
—*Corey's mailman*

INTRODUCTION

Until a few years ago, I was spending over 90% of my time talking about how to get your songs recorded by artists: my favorite musical subject. It slowly came to my attention that the sync world offers a lot more opportunities at a much higher average payment. I am by no means an expert in this area (or any other for that matter). I am grateful to say, however, that I have had a good bit of success in this market recently. I'd love to share with you the knowledge I have picked up and give you the tools to accomplish things you may not have been able to otherwise.

I have put together a Q&A to help explain some of the basics. If nothing else, I hope you get a good laugh or two and then use the pages of the book as toilet paper if needed. As usual, there is a slight chance that a sarcastic, useless answer may preface the correct answer. I'm not sure how that happens. I take life seriously . . . at least twice a year.

May God bless you on your writing journey, and I'm thankful that you are attempting to read this on purpose. Don't forget to check out the original *Hit Happens* for beginning songwriters and *101 Ways to Get Your Songs Recorded*, which are both available on Amazon.

AUTHOR'S SUGGESTION

Keep in mind that every rule of thumb is subject to being broken. We all have our unique characteristics that make us who we are, and that may very well be what opens the door to selling a song in an unconventional manner. Also, remember that talent is a very small part of it. The music business is all about relationships and trust.

Show them that you are organized, prompt, professional, patient, and capable of consistently delivering the goods. If that doesn't work . . . cheat, steal, lie, or go to court and officially change your name to George Lucas. It's like the old saying: "The early bird gets the weasel."

ONE MORE AUTHOR'S SUGGESTION

Don't put your corn dog in the microwave for thirteen minutes. Don't ask me how I know.

What is sync anyway?

A sync is the big white square in your bathroom where you skeet out the leftover food particles nestled between your teeth. Please rinse afterwards or your family will not be happy.

Sync is the term that applies to the synchronization of music with a piece of visual media.

Why should I occasionally take time away from writing for artists to shift my focus to sync?

First of all, why are you writing for artists at all? People who paint pictures often find music distracting and don't have good voices anyway.

This morning, I took a look at RowFax (rowfax.com), which only slightly changes with new info from week to week. If you are not familiar with RowFax, it is the Nashville pitch sheet that tells you which artists are looking for songs at the moment and sometimes even where to send your music. I tallied up the number of opportunities and found 139 artists listed.

According to a reputable source, in the past few years, the number of song placement chances in the sync world has risen to eight million annually. You heard me correctly: eight *million* opportunities per year to get your music in TV, film, ads, video games, and so on. Those are astonishing odds when compared to artist cuts. I wonder which makes the most sense to concentrate on.

What are the differences in payments between sync and artist cuts?

Artists seldom like to cut their hair, while sinks don't have any.

Obviously, the answer varies from case to case. A number-one song by a country or pop artist *could* be in the seven-digit figures, if you are lucky. Realistically, though, you are much more likely to get an indie artist cut than a number-one major artist radio hit. For an average indie artist cut, you will be mailing out a mechanical license for one thousand units, which would be a $91 pre-pay. This $91 would be split between you, the co-writers, and all the publishers. Congratulations: you can now supersize your fries today.

Placing a song in a TV show or movie typically means a sync fee of several hundred or even several thousand dollars up front. More importantly, you also get paid on the back end by your PRO every single time the song airs on TV.

Should I include in my pitch what my normal fee is for using my song?

Yes. Also include that you would like seven bags of multicolored M&M's, minus the blue ones. Let them know that you would like to be a part of the mixing process so you can oversee how your song is being treated and that you will require a trailer with a working shower and low-fat vanilla lattes every other hour between back massages.

Absolutely not. The music supervisor will let you know what the budget is, and then it's up to you to want to be a part of the project or not. Music supervisors don't enjoy having to haggle and renegotiate, as their time is precious and limited. I'm of the "Where do I sign?" mindset so they will remember how easy I was to work with and want to come to me again in the future.

What is a PRO?

PRO stands for Previously Retro Orangutan. Seriously, it's a thing. In the early '90s, there was a movement amongst the South African orangutans to dress in '70s fashion and roller-skate through small jngle villages on Thursdays, with jam boxes on their shoulders, blaring Bee Gees music, in an attempt to keep disco alive. Wait, did I say jingle *villages? I meant to say* jungle *villages. I'm gonna make a note to correct this before we go to print. I don't want anyone thinking I can't spel.*

It should be noted that you can still see the PRO movement happening today from time to time, but they have switched to Tuesdays because it interfered with Bingo night.

Your PRO is your collector of all live performance and airplay royalties. In The US, BMI, ASCAP, and SESAC are your go-to agencies. They are responsible for monitoring the airplay and live performances of your music, collecting the royalties, and paying the publishers and songwriters accordingly.

Please keep in mind that they are not responsible for keeping up with your mechanical licenses or albums sold. To collect earned money for physical copies, you need to do it yourself (or get an administrator). It's like the old saying: "Money is the root of all elves."

***Random shout-out to my buddy Michael August Walton for getting one of his songs placed in the hit series *Shameless*.

How does my PRO know I have a song coming out in a movie or TV show?

One of the main requirements for being a PRO is having psychic ability. Yours will usually have all the info logged into the system before you even finish writing the song, so you have absolutely nothing to worry about. Continue eating your Cheetos in a stress-free manner.

The music supervisor of the show should provide you with a cue sheet to submit to your PRO. Typically they will turn it in themselves, but to be safe, it is always wise to check. I have found instances before where it was not turned in, and I would not have been paid if it weren't for my due diligence.

So what is a cue sheet?

In ancient times, somewhere off the border of Greece and Kentucky, there was a young emperor named Cue. Cue was perfect in every way except one: he was a bed wetter. This very much troubled Cue, as he was soon to be married and obviously did not want his future wife to catch wind of this (no pun intended). Cue hired his cousin Merlin's brother's best friend's neighbor to cast a spell over a special sheet soaked in a Febreze-like substance and sprinkled with the essence of Charmin TP and honeysuckle DNA. The result was an ultra-absorbent, impenetrable super blanket that came to be known as a Cue sheet. Cue went on to have a wonderful marriage and lived happily ever after, even though he continued to have bowel movements on a nightly basis. Long live the Cue!

It should be noted that Cue's cousin Merlin's brother's best friend's neighbor also came up with a dutch oven sheet a few years later, which became the best-selling gag gift at Christmas for many moons to come. He was a very talented fellow.

A cue sheet is a log of all the music used in a particular production. The cue sheet often includes things like this:

01 - Series Film Title
02 - Episode title
03 - Episode number
04 - When the show airs
05 - Length of show
06 - Song title
07 - Who wrote the songs and their PROs
08 - Usage link of each song
09 - Production company of series
10 - What time in the show the song appears

You said the music supervisor should provide me with a cue sheet. What is a music supervisor?

A music supervisor, or MS, is someone hired by the manager to make sure the elevator music continues to play as the hotel guests are pushing the buttons. Imagine walking into an elevator prepared to hear your favorite Dan Fogelberg or Yanni hit and all you hear is silence. Hotel managers are very aware of the catastrophe this could lead to. Since they are too busy setting up the complimentary breakfast buffet, they hire music supervisors to take trips up and down the elevator every thirty minutes and supervise the music. If you are lucky enough to see one, please thank them for their service.

A music supervisor is the person responsible for delivering all the music options for the show or movie. In many cases, they are working on more than one show at a time, so these gatekeepers should be treated like royalty if you get a chance to converse with one. Music supervisors are extremely busy and don't have time to deal with people who don't know the ins and outs of delivering music properly. They each have their preferred methods of delivery, and there is no skipping around that, even if it means more tedious work for you.

Make sure all of your metadata is tagged in the MP3. If they ask for WAV files, you will need to send split sheets, since metadata does not save when WAV files are sent. I repeat: any metadata you've tagged into a WAV file will disappear when you send it. I learned this the hard way. Only send what they ask for, in the format that they ask for it, or you *will* blow your opportunity.

What is metadata?

Metadata is an annual tradition where previous orphans get together and encourage current orphans to be patient and hopeful. It's typically a three-hour event where the previous orphans get up and share their triumphant stories about the glorious day when their search ended and they finally metadata.

Metadata refers to all the underlying information tagged to a song that tells the music supervisor who owns it, controls it, performs it, and the like. Typical things you would find in the metadata would include the following:

- Artist
- Artist picture
- Writers (and their PROs/IPI numbers/percentage of ownership)
- Publishers (and their PROs/IPI numbers/percentage of ownership)
- Track owner
- Controller (go to contact person)

- Email
- Phone number
- Lyric
- BPM
- Year of release

How do I tag this metadata in my MP3?

Can you repeat the question? When you said "MP3," it made me think of C3PO. That took my mind on a rabbit trail to Return of the Jedi, *which made me wonder what would happen if Chewbacca married an Ewok. Could they make it work, or would it be physically impossible? I'm sure we've all had that question from time to time.*

You can easily look up a YouTube video to show you how to do this on whatever type of computer you are working on. Since Mac seems to be the most popular songwriter computer, that's what we'll talk about. To add your metadata, follow these steps:

1. Pull up your iTunes.
2. Single-click to highlight the song you would like to insert your metadata info into.
3. Hit Command and I at the same time.
4. When the magical screen you didn't know existed pops up, fill in every text field so the music supervisor will have no question who owns what or how to contact you.

How do I go about finding email addresses for music supervisors?

The easiest way is to put an ad on Craigslist that says, "Hey, music supes out there, I'm looking to connect and send you some super-cool tracks I made on GarageBand last night in five minutes. I like long walks on the beach and Skee-Ball. I have songs about love, zombies, superhero chicks, and sideways time travel. Be sure to hit me up quick or you'll miss out." You should have no problem.

Here's how to do it:

1. Google can be your best friend and is often the simplest way to find a music supervisor. Let's say your favorite show is *The Walking Dead*. Sometimes it's as simple as typing "who is the music supervisor for walking dead" into a search engine and the name pops up.

2. LinkedIn is another great go-to. You may be able to find the music supervisor for a particular film or movie by searching in the same way you did on Google. I have often typed "music supervisor" without anything more specific and sent connection requests to every single one of them until LinkedIn cut me off. I repeated the same process the next day and the next after that. Try it—if they accept, nine times out of ten, you will have access to their email and can make your pitch request.

3. The pre-credits of the movie or TV show you are interested in also usually list the music supervisor,

so have the pause button and a pen ready the next time you watch.

4. Let a publisher do the work for you. There are many publishing companies out there who have established great connections with the movie industry over the years. If you can get in the door and let them do their magic, you could be way better off than going it alone. Even if you had to give up some of your publishing rights to get it done, 50% of *something* is better than 100% of *nothing*. That's one of the biggest clichés in the business, but it's true. Another bonus could be that they want to hear more of your tunes, and this leads to a publishing deal.

***Random shout-out to Joe Slyzalia for getting a song placed in *Cobra Kai* Season 3. I am officially jealous because I love that show. Congrats, my friend!

How do I learn more about the music supervisor so I can make my pitch request a bit more personal?

Old-fashioned stalking, my friend. Find out where the nearest Waffle House is to their office, and hide behind the jukebox for as many days as it takes. When they finally come in and drop their quarter, you will know what kind of music they are into. Plus, you will be hungry after your long wait and only five steps away from the All-Star Special. Win-Win.

IMDB is a wonderfully informative resource. It stands for Internet Movie Database. This site can also be helpful in locating the music supervisor if you didn't have any luck on LinkedIn or Google. Type in the name of the TV show or film you want to learn about. You will usually find a ton of information about the film, including the following:

- Cast
- Production Crew
- Music Supervisor
- Plot summaries
- RatingsReviewsPersonal
- Bios
- Production status (i.e., preproduction, postproduction, or completed)

Sometimes, in order to find out who is in charge of the music, you'll have to click on the "full cast and crew" link to expand what you originally see and get to the bottom of things. The music supervisor listing is often one of the last things to appear.

You can also search for a music supervisor by name and find out what they are known for and what they are working on at the moment.

What is a sync agent?

A sync agent is a secret agent who hails from the secret land of Syncropolis. Syncropolis has an unorthodox method of training their agents, including such activities as shark-fighting, invisible-cloaking, French-kissing gators and the running of the bulls . . . blind-folded. They are the toughest of the tough and in very high demand, qw if you need a spy.

A sync agent in the sync business is very similar to a song plugger in the artist-pitching business. They typically spend their time working your song for you with the intention of getting the placements you want in exchange for a negotiated percentage of the sync fee. The percentage varies from person to person, but a 50/50 split is common and, in my opinion, fair. You would not have that placement without their efforts, and you would typically still own all your publishing.

Note: There are some sync agents and music libraries that also want half the publishing off their placement and may also want to do a re-title.

What the heck is a re-title?

Re-title is the term given when a world champion thumb wrestler has a major injury and has to relinquish the belt but then, against all odds, is able to win the title again down the line. Thus, it's a re-title.

Let's say you have a song called "The Big Blue Shoe" that someone is representing for you, and that person lands a sync placement for you in the new hit series *Shoeville*. The sync agent, if they had a re-title clause in the contract, could register the song again as "Blue Shoe" so it has a different title. This way, they could participate in the publishing of this placement, but they would not participate if Miley Cyrus cut "Big Blue Shoe" down the line or if it was placed in a different TV show.

The PROs don't have a way of separating different versions of songs. You can imagine what a nightmare it could be if you had a song placed with ten different shows and eight different artists and you worked out different pub splits with each deal.

How do I know my music is right for the TV show I love?

Are you kidding me? That's like asking how I know the Rock would beat Mr. Bean in a kickboxing contest. Of course your music is right. Look who wrote it!

There is a wonderful free site available to you called Tunefind. Simply go to tunefind.com, type in the name of the TV show you want to research, and press enter. Every song they have ever placed on the show will pop up, and you can stylistically compare them to the ones you had in mind. There is no reason to just assume your music is right on target when you can actually use a tool like this to verify that assumption. Give them as few reasons to say no as possible.

Is a music supervisor the only way to get my music used in TV and film?

It's like the old saying: "There's more than one way to skin a coat." My foolproof method consists of finding the address of the production house and sending them my song on a nice cassette tape, along with a fresh bottle of Boone's Farm and a picture of me sunbathing in a rainbow-colored Speedo clutching an ice cream sandwich. It's all about thoughtfulness and packaging. I like to go above and beyond whenever possible.

Not at all. Another popular way to get your music out there is through music libraries. Music libraries are companies that stockpile your music and represent it in negotiations for sync deals. They do this in either exclusive deals for a certain length of time or nonexclusive deals where you can also keep the same songs in other catalogs. Personally, I prefer nonexclusive deals so all my eggs are not in one basket. There are a plethora of opportunities out there and a ton of people who can work your songs, all of which have different contacts. It is very difficult to know who to put your faith in, so choose wisely, and always make sure there is a reversion clause so you are not tying up your song forever.

In case it helps, I've listed a few music libraries you may want to check into, but be aware there are many, many more out there.

- Affix Music
- Airbit
- Artlist
- AudioMicro
- Audio Network
- Audiosocket
- Broadjam
- Directional Music
- Epidemic Sound
- Imaginary Friends Music Partners
- Jamendo
- Jingle Punks
- Marmoset
- Musicbed
- MusicSupervisor.com
- Music Vine
- Nightingale Music
- NOMA Music
- Pond5
- PremiumBeat

- Ricall Music Supervision
- Rumblefish
- RX Music
- Scout Music
- Sentric Music
- Simply Grand Music
- Songtradr
- Soundreef
- Soundstripe
- Sound Lounge
- Storyblocks Audio
- TAXI
- Transition Music Corporation
- YouLicense

What kind of subject matter is best to write about if I want to maximize my chances of placements?

It's best to send songs about your grandma because everyone loves grandma songs. If you don't have any grandma songs, then songs about Ethiopia in June would be cool, because that hasn't been overdone. Everybody has party and love songs. Be unique and send them something that will get their wheels turning, like songs about deaf lamas or drunk squirrels. Think outside of the box, people. You can do this!

I'm glad you asked because that is very important. If you think "universal themes," you will be just fine. For example, how many movies start out with a road trip song with titles similar to "Vacation USA," "We're on Our Way," and "Did Somebody Say Road Trip?"

Here are other examples of things that happen often in movies:

- Championship song (this is my moment)
- Best day ever
- Wedding
- Funeral
- EDM dance songs (for the club)
- Spooky background music (horror movies or mysteries)
- Hype music
- Falling in love
- Heartbreak moment
- Christmas music (between Hallmark and Lifetime alone, there were seventy new Christmas movies made last year)

The more specific you make your song, the higher the chance that you are painting yourself out of a scene.

What are some examples of moods that my music should portray in order to maximize my opportunities for sync placements?

PMS is always the best mood for optimal listening. It makes the listener feel uncomfortable and yet long for more, much like driving by a train wreck and not being able to look away. It's like the old saying: "What doesn't kill you makes you stranger."

For the best placement opportunities, try to hit these common emotions with your music:

- Anthemic
- Happy
- Angry
- Humorous
- Hyped
- Romantic
- Whimsical
- Triumphant
- Sadness/depression
- Inspiring
- Quirky
- Seductive
- Joyful
- Optimistic
- Reflective
- Terrified

Notice that these are all universal feelings that show up over and over in movie scenes and can be written about in vague lyrics.

***Random fact: Up-tempo music is used more often than slower tracks. Bring the energy!!

What if my music has explicit lyrics?

It's a more laid-back world than it used to be. Most parents let their kids sing Snoop Dogg lyrics on TikTok now while smoking a fat one, so I wouldn't worry too much about that. Keep it real, and don't compromise your right to offend old people who wear their socks with their sandals and rock out to The Partridge Family *soundtracks.*

Explicit lyrics will limit your chances to R-rated movies and TV shows. Always record a clean version of your songs for backup so you have options. Most networks have strict guidelines with no wiggle room. Hallmark, Disney, and Nickelodeon, for instance, are not very embracive of swear words for some strange reason. Comedy Central and Cinemax After Dark, on the other hand, may love you.

Can I license a beat rather than an entire song?

\+ prefer prunes, but if you want to license a beat, make sure you work with a farmer who is reasonable in their pricing. Obviously, if it's around Thanksgiving time, there will be a chance you'll get price-gouged because of supply and demand. On the flip side, licensing the prunes after a big meal like that can be dangerous and lead to more trips to the dollar store for toilet paper. Sometimes you can't win.

Yes, beat licensing is not uncommon. It's more likely that an artist, rather than a TV show, will license your beat for their song. Some producers have a page on their website for beats they have created for this very reason, and they will issue a nonexclusive license to the artist for the use of it. If you're good and quick at creating beats, this may be something to strongly consider doing in addition to all the other things you do.

Should I concentrate on the genre I do best or branch out?

It depends on what you do best. If what you do best is burp the alphabet, then I would not concentrate on that. I don't think that will get you many sync placements, although there could be a fraternity movie where that comes in handy.

It only makes sense to be as versatile as possible. If you only write one genre, the briefs will sometimes come in, and you will have absolutely nothing that fits anything. I've literally seen a brief ask for a retro world dance beat with Chinese lyric featuring a drum solo. If you only write country or R&B, you will be scratching your head. Think of how many genres are floating around:

- Ambient
- Big band
- Blues
- Christian (contemporary, Christian country, gospel, Southern gospel)
- Christmas
- Children's
- Classical
- Country
- Disco
- Dubstep
- EDM
- Folk
- Funk
- Grunge
- Heavy metal
- Hip-hop
- Hymn
- Instrumental
- Latin
- Lullaby

- Jazz
- Musical theater
- New Wave
- Opera
- Orchestra
- Pop
- Rap
- Reggae
- Rock (soft, hard, alternative, punk, indie, progressive)
- Ska
- Soul
- Swing
- Techno
- Trance
- World

How many of us have a healthy dose of all of that in our catalog? I'm willing to bet not many, if any. All of those genres will come up from time to time, and we will either be ready or passed over. That's why it pays to co-write with artists and writers of all different styles to help diversify your catalog. Each of us brings a different feel, musically or lyrically, to the table. Let's capitalize off that.

What kind of things should I avoid if I want to keep my lyrics universal?

Honestly, I don't think you should write universal songs. Songs about the universe would probably only fit a sci-fi movie. Who cares about constellations, black holes, aliens, and galaxy quests?

Stick to songs about earth, because at least we've all been there and can relate.

The key is thinking to yourself, "What kinds of things can be too specific and potentially contrast with what a scene might be trying to portray?" Here are some examples:

- Specific cities/states/countries
- Specific bars/restaurants
- Dates
- Colors
- Seasons
- Age of characters
- Time of day

For example, a line like "Blond hair blowin' in the Carolina wind" can be a cool line for country music, but for sync, it can hurt you on many levels.

- If the woman has any hair color other than blond . . . your song doesn't fit.
- If the wind isn't blowing . . . your song doesn't fit.
- If the scene isn't in North or South Carolina . . . your song doesn't fit.

One of my favorite older country songs is a Randy Travis song called "1982." It was great for the '80s, but kids now can't relate because they weren't there. Don't date your song with a date!

How is producing for sync different than producing a demo for an artist pitch?

Producing is tough. I remember when I used to stock produce at a mom-and-pop grocery store. I'm guessing artists would be a little pickier of their produce choices because they are trying to keep in shape. If you're singing for a movie soundtrack, no one sees you, thus your produce choices can be more lax. So there's the difference right there. You're welcome!

If I know an artist well enough, there are times I can send them a work tape and they can hear past the rough spots. If I sent a work tape to a music supervisor, or even a demo for that matter, they may never respond to me again. It is rarely the case that your song will be reproduced unless there is a major soundtrack involved. What you send needs to be professionally mixed and mastered and preferably released as a single. Make sure it is specific to the genre they ask for. If they are requesting authentic blues and the track you sent them fits but the vocalist sounds like Blake Shelton instead of B.B. King, you have missed the mark. Also, make sure the production on your tracks has swells and doesn't just sound the same all the way through. If they aren't really sure when your chorus started, then you aren't doing yourself any favors.

Does it matter if I use a demo singer and unreleased track instead of an artist cut to pitch?

It depends. If you are single and the music supervisor is single, then I would send the version with the ugliest singer to them. The last thing you need is for the music supervisor to fall in love with the singer and have your chances go from one in a million to zero. Don't do that to yourself. Always pick hideous singers and you'll be covered either way. Think smart!

Before Spotify and social media came along, it seemed like hiring great demo singers that sounded like they should be in the movies and producing great tracks to pitch was the thing to do. Nowadays, the music supervisors will likely look up the artist on the submission and check their fan base, Spotify count, and other statistics. If the song submitted has a ton of spins on Spotify, it may bump your song to the top of the wanted list for the placement. Bringing your fans to their film is a smart idea on their part if you have a big following, and a large spin count on your song already saves them the work of market testing.

***Random shout-out to Bill DiLuigi for getting his song "It Turns" placed in the movie *Stars Fell on Alabama*.

In what format should I send my music to be considered?

I find that 8-tracks are the best. People love vintage throwback surprises. Second best would be vinyl. Never pass up a chance to stand out.

Not every music supervisor likes their songs delivered in the same way. Some like to give a first listen by going through links such as SoundCloud or ReverbNation. Some like a Dropbox or zip file containing MP3s. They will eventually need WAV files, but often not for the first listen, as they can take up too much space on their hard drive.

The most popular delivery method lately has been disco.ac. Disco costs me a bit less than two hundred bucks a year, and I can create playlists for whomever I want to send my music to. When the recipient clicks on the song, they can immediately see the lyrics, artist pic, and metadata, so they know they are dealing with an organized, professional person. If they see the lyric is way off target, it saves them from wasting their time listening to the song.

Should I send the tracks without vocals as well?

Yes. If a music supervisor loves your song, they may want to take the track to the karaoke club and sing it that night. If they happen to be there with Beyoncé and she gets up on stage and sings it with them, there could be a viral video in the works. That viral success could prompt Beyoncé, if she's drunk enough, to drive to the studio right away and record it for a future single release. The sky is the limit from there.

Always make sure you include your background tracks without vocals in the delivery. Many music supervisors will not accept the submission without them. The reason being is there could be scenes in the film where the vocals need to be pulled back in certain places so the dialog between the actors can be clearly heard, and this gives them a few options to work with. Honestly, when my first song in a Hallmark Movie was being played, I had to stick my ear to the TV to even hear that it was my song. The fact that they used over two minutes of it for a dinner conversation made up for it, though.

When it comes to lyrics in sync, is it "the more the merrier" or "less is more?"

No need to leave them complaining because they didn't get the whole story. Go ahead and condense three songs into one so they can hear the story of the trilogy and not feel shafted. Think biography, not short poem.

Less is more wins 90% of the time. Sync music is so much more about the vibe the music creates or supports rather than the lyric being the star. Space between lyrics allows more time for dialog to happen, and that's what matters most in film. You may have certain rapid-fire lyrics in dance songs, but typically, letting it breathe gives you more opportunities.

When a production company says the licensing fee is "$1,000 all in," what does "all in" mean?

$1,000 "all in" simply means they put the entire $1,000 all in the envelope they are sending you. Otherwise it would say $1,000 "some in," and they'll mail the rest on Sunday after church.

Typically, when your song gets chosen, two payments will be coming your way:

1. The sync fee (paid for the use of your melody and lyrics synchronized with their visual media)
2. The masters fee (paid for the use of your masters)

"All in" simply means they put both checks together, and whoever controls it on your part will divide it up accordingly. This fee is usually paid upfront as opposed to the performance royalties, which will be collected after it airs and is distributed several months later.

This fee is normally split down the middle. For example, if you agreed to $1,000 "all in," $500 would go to the track owner (whoever paid for the recording), and the other $500 would be split evenly between the publishers and co-writers.

It's important to note that if the track owner was an investor and not a writer or publisher of the song, this is where their monetary gain ends. Publishers and writers, on the other hand, will get paid from their PRO every time the song hits TV.

What kind of factors are involved in determining how much I get paid for a song when it airs from my PRO?

1. *How close you sit from the TV*
2. *How many actors are named Sam*
3. *How many curse words are in French*
4. *Whether the show aired while your PRO was awake*
5. *How old the youngest actress is*
6. *What key your song is in*
7. *Where the publisher went to grade school*
8. *Who shot J.R.*

Your payment will depend on some combination of these factors:

1. How big the network is
2. How many people are watching
3. Whether your song carries the scene or people are talking over it
4. If your song is played over the opening or closing credit or somewhere in-between
5. How much of your song they played
6. Whether it's the theme song

What is the difference between control and ownership of a song?

The publishers and writers "own" the song, and the person or persons that paid for the recording session "own" the masters. They all "control" their ownership portions until such time as they give permission to someone to represent the song for sync pitches, so that it will be clear and ready. It doesn't mean they gave up any ownership; it simply means they are allowing someone to take charge and "control" what happens to the song in the sync world.

If you are personally representing the song, you may send out an email that goes something like the following:

> Hello, [insert name here]. I'm reaching out to see if you're in need of some tagged and cleared music for your new show *When Waffles Attack*. I loved your work on *French Toast Farmers*. I control 200% of each song and always say yes to your budget. My team has previous placements on Animal Planet, *Rocky 85*, and *Better Call Sally*.
>
> Thank you for your time and let me know if I can help in any way,
> Bobby Joe Valentine
> 555-123-4567

Notice a few things that I did in that email:

1. I kept it short and to the point.

2. I let him know I did my homework and I'm familiar with his previous work.
3. I let him know that he only has to go through me because I control 200% (the song and the masters).
4. I let him know that the metadata is taken care of so he knows he's dealing with a professional.
5. I let him know that I'm trying to fill a need he may have rather than saying gimmie, gimmie, gimmie ("what can you do for me?").

It's very important to be looked at as someone who wants to help fill a void rather than someone reaching for handouts. There's a big difference in the perception of those two things.

It's expensive to produce songs for sync! Any ideas on how I can cut costs when producing my future cinematic masterpieces?

One way to save money on production is to have an all-day session where you can track ten songs; pay all the musicians, singers, and producers with checks; and then immediately move two states away before the checks bounce. But I heard from a friend that might not be the most ethical way. I'll try to get a second opinion.

1. Have an artist in the room. I almost always have an artist in the room when I write in hopes that they will want to record the song for their project and pitch to sync as well. It's a double blessing if all goes well.

2. Co-write. I co-write twice a day, every day. If you don't have that option, another thing you can do is have co-writing sessions with two or three (or twenty-seven) other people. This way, you can divide the expense among you as well as increase the pitching efforts.
3. Write with a producer/track builder. There have been times when I have offered equal songwriter credit to a track builder in order to get the song marketable. It's worth it, in my opinion, even if they can't add anything as a writer, because sync is so much about the feel. I'd rather be a small part of something amazing than 100% writer on something I can't pitch.

What does "clear" mean?

Clear is the term happy teenagers yell when the final zit has been removed from their face in plenty of time for prom pictures.

Clear means that all parties involved in the creation, ownership, and recording of the song have agreed that you can say yes to whatever deal is offered. It's almost like a power of attorney, so to speak, for the song.

Imagine for a minute that a song was co-written by five people and they all had publishing deals. A music supervisor doesn't have time to call five publishers, five writers, and the track owner to explain the offer to each of them and see if they agree. It's one person in charge or on to someone else with an easier scenario.

I've heard sometimes the MS asks for the stems as well. What are stems?

You know how there are times when you have a pimple that comes out of nowhere just before your wedding day? The stem is the tiny piece that supports the white pus that you will soon be launching into the atmosphere by squeezing your fingers around it. I'm not really sure why someone would request that, but it's important not to judge. It's in the Bible. So, there's that.

Stems are basically sub mixes of fuller mixes. For instance, you could have a mix of the bass and drums, then a separate mix of keys and guitar, a vocal mix, and so on. They are subsection mixes that, when played at full volume together, make up a full mix.

The producer may have loved the song but thought the instrumentation was too heavy and wanted a more stripped-down version. This gives them something to play with if they have the time. It's a good idea to have the stems available, in addition to the full mix, in case they ask for them.

***Random shout-out to my buddy Shantell Ogden for getting her song "Countdown to Christmas" placed in the upcoming movie *Christmas Retreat*.

Who needs to sign off on a form to make sure the song is clear for me to pitch?

1. *Your dog*
2. *The postman*
3. *The teller at your bank*
4. *Your second-grade teacher*
5. *The lunch lady*
6. *Any former NFL player*
7. *Whoever is standing behind you right now*

In a perfect world, this is who should sign off:

1. All publishers
2. All writers
3. All musicians
4. The producer
5. The engineer
6. All background singers
7. The track owner

That sounds like way too much work. Why do we need to do all that?

You don't. Just do the pinkie promise thing and that should stand up in court. No need to cross your i's or dot your t's. That's what people who don't believe in Netflix do. Suckers!

Music supervisors have to cover their butts. Sometimes a writer or publisher wants the cut so bad that they just assume/hope/pray the offer is OK with everyone else when it actually isn't. This creates a potential lawsuit if the movie comes out when the permission to use that song wasn't granted by one angry publisher who thought it was worth $5,000 instead of the $500 that was offered.

Also, from a musician standpoint, the pay scale is different for a demo than it is for a master session. They may have accepted the lower payment, not knowing you were pitching it to sync, but they could demand the difference after the song makes it out there.

Do I have to be a famous singer to get sync placements?

Yes. Would you rather watch a movie where Norah Jones sings the wedding song or your uncle Frank?

Not hardly. Most films don't have the budget to license Snoop Dogg or Metallica songs. The indie artists are much more likely to be budget friendly and say yes to whatever is offered. Personally, I try to always work with a music supervisor's budget, even if I think it's worth more. My hope is that they will remember me next time and keep coming back to the well.

I had someone represent me once for a big movie placement. They ended up asking for more than was offered, and we lost the deal. I'm determined to never let that happen again.

What are some of the biggest challenges to getting sync placements?

1. *Most people already have a sink*
2. *They are very heavy to carry*

There are so many challenges I don't know where to start, but here goes:

1. You're competing with music libraries.
2. You're competing with other fantastic writers.
3. Most music supervisors are in LA, New York, or Canada. It's hard to have coffee with them or take them out to lunch to get to know them when you live anywhere else.
4. They have a circle of friends they already trust, and it's hard to break through.

5. Some production houses have their own music departments that create all their material.
6. Many music supervisors are writing most of the songs they are submitting themselves. (That's why collaborating with one is extremely helpful if you get the chance. Your chances of success increase exponentially. It's the same concept as writing with the producer or the actual artist when you are trying to get a cut on their album, which I typically do every time I write.)

***Random tip: Write with recording artists as much as possible. Not only does it increase your chances of getting a song on their album, but their recording of your song is more ammunition for pitching that you didn't have to pay for, provided that they give you permission to represent the song for sync purposes.

About how many scripted shows per year are being produced in the United States?

One.

In 2019, there were 532. This does not include reality shows, game shows, sporting events, and the like. COVID played a factor in bringing the number down in 2020, but it seems to be increasing every year with new shows pooping up all over the place. I mean *popping*. Shows do not poop.

How many songs does the average movie use?

I don't know. You should watch all of them and count . . . in Spanish. Then divide by 11.

It's a pretty broad range. Some use a dozen and some use over thirty. Obviously, movies that involve dancing, cheerleading or athletic competitions, or recording artists chasing careers will be on the higher end. I believe there were at least two and a half songs in the *Pitch Perfect* films. Action movies tend to use more high-energy, non-lyrical EDM music, but there are exceptions to every rule.

How do I register the split percentage if I write most of the song and my co-writer adds some here and there?

Multiply the number of writers by the publisher's street address. Divide that number by 3 and then add the number of second chorus words to the number of bridge syllables. Subtract that by 6 and you're golden.

Unless you have a prior arrangement or understanding with each other, it's always an equal split when you walk into a writing room, regardless of how much of whose words or melody you end up using. This is always the way I have approached it to be fair. You may have kicked butt today, but your co-writer may be in the zone on the next one. It all evens out in the wash, as they say. Don't lose your friendships over silly disputes built off syllable counts. If the song is already done and they are able to change a line or two that makes it better, then perhaps a smaller percentage could be offered. Otherwise, sharing is caring . . . or some other similar quote that John Wayne would never say.

How can I utilize my past successes to get future placements?

Lie. Invent your current placements and lie as if they are your previous placements, and that should lead to your future placements. Fake it until you make it.

One thing that has helped me tremendously has been creating banners with collages of TV shows that have used my songs. I've done the same thing with artists who have recorded them. A banner like that in your email signature shows the music supervisor that you have had previous successes, so you are probably worth a listen. If you notice, I also listed some of them in my introductory email, so they have two ways of noticing that I've had good things happen before.

What if I haven't had any placements before and only my co-writer has?

It's probably because you suck. Kidnap your co-writer and assume their identity. If they are a true friend, they will understand.

The funny thing is, even if I didn't have any placements, I could still use the exact sample of the introductory email that I would have used if it were me who had the placements. Remember, my last line of the email was "My team has previous placements on Animal Planet, *Rocky 85*, and *Better Call Sally*." As long as someone in your team accomplished these things, it's still true. They don't care which one of you had placements or cuts. They only need to know someone did.

Is there anything I can do as a musician to make sure my songs are as worthy of sync placements as possible?

Yes. Always play in the key of R, and don't tune up, because that is way too predictable. Definitely start your song with a riff from any Eagles hit, because they will recognize it and immediately be hooked. I heard from this guy at Shoney's Buffet who lives next door to a lawyer's grandpa that it's only copyright infringement if you play it in the same key, so R is always safe.

For one thing, I would learn as many chords as possible. If you only know the basic major chords you will quite possibly cut yourself out of most sad or scary songs, as they often revolve around dark, minor chords. The more versatile you are with your chord patterns and voicings, the more likely you are to land placements in different genres. Major chords can be great for country, Americana and blues, but have you ever heard a John Mayer song that simply used G, C, and D?

It should be noted that major chords are useful, however, in the up-tempo happy songs. So don't feel like you need to avoid them all together. "Achy Breaky Heart" sold over 9 million copies and only had two chords. In fact, that song never even changed melodies when it hit the chorus. Was that song a huge sync song? No. So, why am I bringing it up? I have no idea. I ran out of coffee thirty minutes ago.

What are some things music supervisors love?

1. *When you call them every day to make sure they heard your material.*
2. *When you send them 7 MP3's per email, with no metadata attached.*
3. *When you send copies of you shredding the Fender into your computer with a note that says "Imagine this with a full band and Slash as lead guitarist".*
4. *When they ask for a pop song and you send them bluegrass.*
5. *When you say the song is clear and forget that the other two writers have publishing deals.*
6. *When they ask to hear your three best songs, and you send them a zip file of everything you recorded since 1985.*
7. *When you save money by not using professional vocalists and sing it yourself, in one take, with no tuning.*
8. *When you include samples of songs that are not public domain and don't mention that.*
9. *When you drive to their house, camp in their yard, hold a jam box above your head like John Cusack, and play your originals as loud as possible.*
10. *When you ask if they have a Tinder account.*

Is there such a thing as being too on the nose when it comes to titles?

Michael Jordan won six titles. I have a feeling that doesn't answer the question, but I really like Michael Jordan. Larry Bird won three before his back gave out, but he could've and should've won more. So, there's that.

The best example of that I can think of is *The Walking Dead*. I had a friend who knew another friend of an acquaintance who said he had the perfect song for *The Walking Dead*. It was called "Zombies on the Rise."

Why is that wrong? In the entire saga of *The Walking Dead*, I have never heard them mention the word *zombie* ever, nor do they sing about what's going on at the moment. In fact, there are very few actual songs with lyrics in that show. It's more of a mood music series.

That being said, I'd be lying if I said that as soon as the Hallmark titles are announced before production, I don't try to write as many of them as possible on the off chance that I could land a theme song to one of them.

I co-wrote the theme songs for *Tom's Wild Life* on GAC and *Last Chance Highway* on Animal Planet with Lucas Hoge, and the titles of the songs were the exact titles of the TV show. Thus, sometimes it's OK to be on the nose and sometimes it's not. It's like the old saying: "You never know until you tricycle."

Is there a music supervisor directory that can shorten my search?

No. You used to be able to find one on the second shelf at Larry's Used Books and Tacos in New York, but when Larry passed away, he forgot to tell the owner who checked it out last. He also forgot to tell him who the vendor was for their tacos, so they closed a week later. Larry is and will always be missed. We love you, Larry!

One free directory that can be helpful is songwriteruniverse.com. It focuses on the US, Canada, and the United Kingdom. If your vocals are in English, that's a great place to start.

Once I sign the sync license agreement, does that guarantee it will be in the movie or TV show?

Duh. What part of "signed agreement" do you not understand?

Unfortunately, it does not. It stands a good chance, but sometimes they have to secure the agreement simply to know that you agree on the price, should it be the perfect fit. Think of it more like a letter of intent. I have had songs bumped from movies at the last minute more than once. The good thing is, if the MS liked your song enough to send you a license agreement, then it will remain on their radar for future similar movies they may be working on.

How long will it take to get paid when I get a placement?

My grandfather had an old saying. Well, it wasn't that old, but it was a saying. Actually, it wasn't a saying, it was more like a philosophy. This philosophy really said it all. Unfortunately, I can't remember what it was or if it even related to the question. He did really like Mexican food, though, for whatever that's worth.

The sync fee usually comes in before or shortly after the song airs. The back pay from your PRO, however, is normally nine months behind, much like radio play.

I've tried to skip all those steps and reach out to co-write with professional writers who are already

plugged in. Why don't they answer my emails in a timely manner? Are all successful writers jerks?

Yes. Only a complete self-absorbed butthead would refuse to cancel or turn down meetings with other equally in-demand writers to write with someone who has no track record, connections, publishing deal, or recording career. I mean, where do they get off making business decisions like that? It's absolutely preposterous, if you ask me.

Too often in Nashville, new writers, or even writers who have been at it for a while, get frustrated at the lack of interest from writers who are perceived as more successful than they are. It doesn't mean that those writers are inconsiderate or egocentric. It simply means there are only so many hours in the day for a hit writer to impress the powers that be and keep their jobs. It is in their best interest to choose their co-writers as wisely as possible. In many cases, they don't even get to choose, as their publishing company may wish to control 100% of the publishing on every song.

Other than having their core friend group already set, there are many reasons they may not have time to squeeze you in, and I thought this list may help shed some light on the type of co-writers they look for in order of importance. Many of them never look past #6.

1. Famous artists who are currently looking for songs for their next album
2. Famous artists who are not looking yet but regularly record
3. Hit writers with staff deals who are currently on a hot streak

4. Old-school legends who may end up doing another album one day
5. Hit writers without current staff deals
6. Recording artists who aren't famous yet but have a big following and are on the cusp of a deal (currently recording)
7. New staff writers without cuts yet but who are signed to a pub deal with a successful song plugger attached
8. Recording artists who aren't famous yet but have a big following, are currently on the cusp of a deal, but are not looking for songs yet
9. Recording artists who are not known yet but are currently looking for songs for an album
10. Singer-songwriters with in-house studios who are great at vocals and mixing
11. Songwriters with in-house studios who are great with mixing but don't sing
12. Rich co-writers who can pay for demos
13. Fantastic singers (so at least they could pitch the work tape if there is no demo money)
14. Songwriters who don't sing or barely play an instrument but seem nice

The harsh reality is that most of us fall in category 14 or 13 at best, which makes for a tremendous battle in gaining the attention of a professional writer. It doesn't mean it's impossible, but it does make sense for us to not be so offended when we don't get the response we hoped for. Hang in there, keep improving, and refuse to give up, no matter what the odds!

Seven places to not eat a Pop-Tart:

1. In your bathroom
2. In your underwater
3. Next to someone on a diet
4. In my bathroom
5. At a funeral
6. Standing next to a starving dog
7. In anyone else's bathroom

***Random shout-out to these great organizations:**

- **Simply Grand Music**
- **Ohana Music Group/CCB Nashville**
- **Nashville Records**
- **Granite Records/March Family Music**
- **Stockbridge Records**
- **Songs of Hookline**
- **MC1 Nashville Music Publishing**

All these companies at one time or another have allowed me to come on board as a staff writer, creative director, or both. Without the free time to create, it would have been impossible to accomplish half the things I've been blessed to be a part of. I am grateful to you and all of my fans (both of them) who have believed in me from the start. Thank you from the bottom of my heart . . . . . and the top . . . . . and the middle!

Thanks to COVID-19, I don't know where I'll end up next, but I am extremely grateful for that company as well. I choose to act on faith! —CLB (5-24-21)

In Closing

I want to reiterate what I said in the first book. My three rules for success are:

1. Persistence
2. Persistence
3. More persistence

I know what it's like to do all of the following:

1. Audition for a place to play original music and fail
2. Get fired from a place I was playing for free (great confidence builder)
3. Send songs to music supervisors and fail
4. Send songs to artists and fail
5. Reach out to more successful writers for co-writes and fail
6. Enter song contests and fail
7. Write ten songs for a specific commercial and fail
8. Write over one hundred Christmas songs in one year to pitch to Hallmark and fail all one hundred times
9. Write a song with a famous artist on their tour bus two hours before their recording session and fail to get it on the album
10. Have songs on hold for megastars and have them pass away before studio day
11. Reach out to every publishing company I can find and fail

As a matter of fact, I pitch 3,000 times a year on average. That's artists and TV/film combined. My most successful year, numbers wise, was this past year, when I got 90 cuts/placements. I am extremely grateful for those 90 cuts, and it's wonderful to be able to say I accomplished that. However, if you do the math of me failing 2,910 times, that means I'm about a 97% failure on my best year. Let that sink in for a moment. It's all about perspective. Am I gonna focus on all the misses and whine, or am I gonna be totally stoked about the ones that found their homes? I choose option 2 every day of my life.

If any of this helped you in your career, I'd love to hear about it. Shoot me an email at coreyleebarkertunes@gmail.com and let me know your success stories. I am pulling for you!

10 Questions for the Author

1. What was your first ever sync placement?

In 2005, Lucas Hoge, Brent Anderson, and myself wrote a song for *Smallville* from Clark Kent's point of view to Lana Lang. He wanted to tell the secret of who he was but knew it could be dangerous. The song was called "If Only I Could." Initially, the music supervisor said he liked it but would have to find the perfect spot for it to work. We waited on pins and needles for six months until he emailed and said, "You might want to turn on your TVs Thursday night and tune in." It was a huge blessing because it happened to be my favorite show at the time.

2. Have you ever been the artist on one of your sync placements?

Not officially. However, there is a Halloween song I sang called "Boneyard Boogie" that is, as of this publication, on hold for a Halloween documentary series. If we get lucky and that goes through, it will be my first. I wrote it with the music supervisor Donna Britton and producer/buddy/neighbor David Norris. Great folks!

3. What's your favorite genre to write for in the sync world?

I write over one hundred Christmas songs every year to chase Hallmark, Lifetime, and recording artists, so that's an easy answer. After the sixth person called me Christmas Corey, I kind of embraced it and even set up a Facebook page for it. That genre has been extremely kind to me. It's very difficult to be known for anything, so I'm grateful so many artists think of me when they want to write for a Christmas album or a movie pitch. I'm ready 365 days a year. Bring on the jelly! I mean the *jolly*.

4. You mentioned RowFax for country artists looking for songs. Is there a similar pitch sheet for TV and film listings?

There are a few out there. The tricky thing is, often when you get a brief in, they need the song that day or the next, as opposed to RowFax, where listings are sometimes posted months in advance. You have to either be a track builder with a lot of free time or already be prepared with your mixed and mastered track. That's why I always think about universal topics when I'm putting sync songs together ahead of time without knowing what the need is. I ask myself, "What need comes up the most? I'll write that!"

5. What's the biggest mistake sync track producers are making these days?

Fake Drums. There are some shows where the song is buried so far beneath the dialog that it won't matter, but I've heard from several music supervisors lately that their biggest pet peeve is great instrumentation ruined by fake drums. Pay for the real thing my friends. It's an easy fix.

6. There were only two years between your first and second books. Why did this one take so long?

I ran out of knowledge.

I didn't feel like I'd put in the years of effort to make enough mistakes to share with the world. I'd been writing for artists my whole life, but sync was too new. I wanted to make sure I had enough wisdom for readers to make it worth their $10 or whatever the publisher charges. I also did a guest lecture at NADU recently, which got me a bit fired up to get it done. Check out Nashville Artist Development University when you get a chance. Kory Brunson and Jason Wyatt are exceptionally good at what they do. They are doing great things for artists and writers at a cost that is affordable and more than worth it!

7. What's the toughest thing about transitioning from writing for artists to writing for sync?

The toughest thing for me personally is that I've spent thirty years building up this massive catalog of country songs, and it's one of the least-used genres in the sync business. There are still some opportunities, but most of the music supervisors are from LA, New York, and Canada. Country is not the first thing they want to hear. Even in the Christmas genre, I've had to swap out some of the country voices for someone that sounds more like Michael Bublé, John Mayer, or Gwen Stefani.

Another tough thing is the additional need for background tracks. Over the years, I've lost a lot of the background tracks in computer crashes, and I often can't make the pitches without them. It's a shame. *Always* keep background tracks, and back them up in more than one place.

8. What's the best thing about writing for sync compared to writing for artists?

In many cases, when an artist cuts a song, whether they are a big artist or an indie, it deters someone else from wanting to record it. This can be upsetting for a writer because that artist may only have a couple fans, meaning 99.99999% of the world never heard the song, and yet other artists are passing it up. In the sync world, a wonderfully produced appropriate tune could land in fifty different places. There is nobody saying, "Oh, we heard that in episode thirty-eight of *Swamp Masters*, so we can't use it." That's a beautiful thing for a content creator.

I'm not sure I've ever seen a movie with a make-out scene that wasn't playing "Let's Get It On" in the background for comical effect. Case in point.

9. Which music supervisor have you worked with the most?

Lately, it has been Donna Britton from Mollygirlmusic.com. She has been very gracious to listen to all kinds of songs I've sent her for projects and even Zoomed in to co-write some. Check out her website when you can to see what she's up to. She's always got something cool cooking!

10. Where can folks hear your music?

If you search YouTube for "corey lee barker tunes," a ton will come up. You can also hear songs that have been recorded by various artists on Spotify from the "Christmas Corey" playlist. Otherwise, try these links:

www.reverbnation.com/christmascorey (for holiday)
www.reverbnation.com/coreyleebarker4/songs (for sync and pop/country)

www.reverbnation.com/coreyleebarker (for inspirational)

www.reverbnation.com/coreycountry (for traditional country)

My hope is that you use this book actively as you get started in your sync career. With this in mind, I am adding a separate section for you to make notes as you write hooks and ideas down for subject matter that keeps on showing up over and over! As you think of titles or interesting lines, jot them down and save them under that heading. This will help keep you organized until you can find time to complete the songs. I do the same thing in my phone memos. It's good to have a physical copy, though, that can't be accidentally deleted. There's nothing worse than having a great idea for your next hit and then forgetting what it was. It's also great to have this when you come into a co-write. It saves a lot of time and shows the other writer or writers that you have done some prep work for the session.

HOOKS/IDEAS FOR ROAD TRIP SONGS

HOOKS/IDEAS FOR LOVE SONGS

HOOKS/IDEAS FOR SPORTS ANTHEMS

HOOKS/IDEAS FOR OVERCOMING OBSTACLES

HOOKS/IDEAS FOR HOLIDAY SONGS

HOOKS/IDEAS FOR WEDDING SONGS

HOOKS/IDEAS FOR DANCE PARTY SONGS

HOOKS/IDEAS FOR DINNER DATE MUSIC

HOOKS/IDEAS FOR HEART BREAK SONGS

HOOKS/IDEAS FOR CHILL MOMENTS

HOOKS/IDEAS FOR HEROS

HOOKS/IDEAS FOR BAD GUYS

HOOKS/IDEAS FOR INSPIRATIONAL SONGS

HOOKS/IDEAS FOR COMEDY/QUIRKY SONGS

HOOKS/IDEAS FOR SEXY MOMENTS

HOOKS/IDEAS FOR NEW ORLEANS JAZZ

HOOKS/IDEAS FOR BLUES CLUB SCENES

HOOKS/IDEAS FOR GOSPEL SONGS (Think Godflix)

HOOKS/IDEAS FOR FOLLOW YOUR DREAM SONGS

HOOKS/IDEAS FOR SCARY SCENES

YOUR IMPORTANT MUSICAL CONTACTS LIST

Name
Email
Phone Number

Name
Email
Phone Number

Name
Email
Phone Number

Name
Email
Phone Number

Name
Email
Phone Number

Name
Email
Phone Number

Name
Email
Phone Number

Name

Email
Phone Number

Name
Email
Phone Number

Name
Email
Phone Number

Name
Email
Phone Number

Name
Email
Phone Number

Name
Email
Phone Number

Name
Email
Phone Number

Lastly, set at least a dozen goals that you would like to see happen in the next year that will help hold you accountable for not slowing down your chase of the dream. I personally set 40, but I drink a lot of coffee! They could be setting the number of songs you want to write or produce, number of music supervisors you plan on reaching out to per month, what you'd like to improve on, new instrument you want to learn, increasing your studio network, how many different genres you will write for, increasing your demo singer contacts, etc.

If you don't write it down, you are less likely to do it!

As a wise poet once said, "Get'r done!"

About the Author

Corey Lee Barker (a.k.a. Christmas Corey) has had over 1000 songs cut by artists or placed in TV shows since his 1998 arrival in Nashville. His music has been placed on ABC, Hallmark, Cinemax, Netflix, *Entertainment Tonight*, Animal Planet, Hulu, WB Network, CW Network, *MLB Tonight*, *The Amazing Race*, *Smallville*, *The Messengers*, *Hope for Christmas*, *Last Chance Highway* (theme song), FDTV, *Tom's Wild Life* (theme song), *Hoge Wild*, *Road to Christmas*, *Hashtag Blessed*, etc.

Artists who have recorded Corey's music include but aren't limited to William Shatner, Vince Gill, Tracy Lawrence, Darryl Worley, Jamie O'Neal, T. G. Sheppard, Neal McCoy, Claudette King (B.B. King's daughter), Cledus T. Judd, Buddy Jewell, Home Free, Daryle Singletary, Pam Tillis, Rebecca Lynn Howard, Bill Anderson, Jeff Bates, Johnny Lee, Jeff Carson, Jesse Keith Whitley, Jeff Cook (of Alabama), Jason Jones (Warner Brothers), Rhonda Vincent, Jeannie Seely, the Jordanaires, Lucas Hoge, and others.

Corey's songs have been on Grammy-winning albums and #1 Billboard albums collectively in Country, Bluegrass, and Polka. Corey has received nominations or wins for Song or Songwriter of the Year multiple times by the ICMA, the Josie Music Awards, the Tennessee Songwriters Association International, the Texas Country Music Association, the World Songwriting Awards, the GMA, the KCMA, and the NACMAI. Be sure to check out Corey's other two books: "Hit Happens" and "101 Ways to Get Your Songs Recorded."

*Thanks again for reading this, my friends!

May God bless you all! —Corey

P.S. If you give this book a perfect rating on Amazon and make a positive social media post about it . . . there is a great chance that you will win a million dollars the next time you buy a gas station lottery ticket. Well, maybe not a great chance, but there's a good chance. Well, maybe not a good chance, but there's a chance. OK, you're probably not gonna win a million dollars. But it would make me feel good, and that's basically the same thing. Basically.
*Update – I landed a new job writing for Diamonds in the Rough Publishing on February 1, 2022 and couldn't be happier. Great things are in the works!

ARTISTS WHO HAVE CUT COREY'S SONGS

Abner Glick

Adam Highbarger

Adam Tucker

Adam Warner

Adrianna Freeman

Adrienne Haupt

Alexandra Mckenna

Alan Turner

Ali Cutter

Allen Mckendree

Allie Sealey

Allison McBryar

Allison Rae

Alisha Rae

Aly Jordan

Alyssa Jacey

Amanda Michaels/Reed Amy Gas

Amy Jones

Amy McAllister

Andres Salgado

Andrew Marshall

Aneesa

Anna Claire

Anna Reynolds

Anna Voorhies

Angie Lynn Carter

Antonio Moreas

Ariela Aspen

Arkin Terrell

Ashley Helmuth

Ashley Strickland

Aubree Bullock

Austin Olvey

Ava Davis

Ava Paige

Baby Band

Barry Michael

Becky Burr

Ben Rives Jr.

Bernadette Kathryn

Berry Preston

Bethany La Deaux

Bill Anderson

Bill Bertrand

Billy Bob Earl

Bill Gaines Blueground & Clara Brad Henley

Brad Tucker

Brandon Lee

Brei Carter

Brent Anderson

Brey Noelle

Bridget Walling

Brody Taylor

Brooke Morton

Brooke Veigas

Brooke Woods Caley

Cal Rudy

Calvin Ray

Cari Lynn York

Carole Champagne

Cash Creek
Chad Bushnell
Chad Cook Band
Charee White
Charles Tham
Chase Truran
Charity Bowden
Chase Tyler
Chelsea Rae
Chloe Jane
Chris Garner
Chris Golden
Chris Lee
Chris Morris
Chuck Hancock
Ciera Mackenzie
Clare Cunningham
Claudette King
Cledus T Judd
Cook & Glenn
Corey Farlow

Cori & Kelly

Cormac Neeson Country Generations

Craig Downey

Curtis Braly

Cynthia Leigh Anne

Damon Hendrix

Dana Davis

Dan Harell

Danny Kensy

Danny Ray Harris

Darren Warren

Dave Emerson

Darryl Worley

Daryl Keith Norman

Dave Adkins

Dave Smith

Danika and the Jeb Danika Portz

David Valesquez

Dawn King

Dawn Rix

Daryle Singletary

DC Riggs

Debbie Anthony Debbie Mills

Delnora Reed

Del Robbins

Dennis Reynolds

Donnie Gene

Donnie Lee Strickland

Doug Mathis

Dustin Chapman

Dusty Leigh

Eddie Arnold

Ellie Rose

Emily Daniels

Emily Faith

Emily Duff

Erin Kelly

Funk-E-Fresh

G2RRL

Gabriella

Gareth Campbell

Garrett Abraham

Garrett Clark

Bell Gary & Kelly Voorhies

Gary Tennison

Gemma Adams

Grace Michelle

Grace Wilson

Gracey Smith

Greg Baggett

Greg Roberts

Haley Mannis

Hannah Anders

Heather Smith

Heather Warren

Hollyann

Home Free

Hugh Alan

Hunter Cook

Hunter May

ICMA All Stars

Isaac Cole

Izabella Damron

Jace Hill
Jackson Forrest
Jada Vance
Jake Aaron Michael
James Cazad
James Lann
James Smith
Jamie O'neal
Janis Japa
Jason Jones
Jason Turner
Jaidyn Laborde
Jay Black
JC Brae
Jeanie Sealey
J Edwards
Jeff Bates
Jeff Burns
Jeff Cook
Jeff Wood
Jenna Faith Oakley

Jenni Dale Lord

Jennifer Moorman

Jenny Bond

Jesse Keith Whitley

Jessica Dean

Jessica Farmer

Jill VanMeter

Jimmy Sturr

Jody Harris

Jody Medford

Joey Hyde

Joe Sly

John Randolph

Johnny Lee

Jon Pat Dickenson

J Scott Evans

Judy Pastor

Julio Reeves

Junior Gordon

Justine Blazer

Justin Love

Justin Ryan

Justin Richardson

Justin Wilson

Kaitlyn Jackson

Kacey Selzer

Kali Rose

Kane and Kelly

Kathryn Shipley

Katie Santiago

Kayla J

Kaytee Ross

Keeley Dodd

Keith Morrison

Kelly Fitzgerald

Kendra Muecke

Kennedy Brady

Kenzie Moody (with Suubi Tribe)

Kerry Randel

Kerstin Scheibel

Kevin Armstrong

Kevin Moynihan

Kevin Woodard

Kezia Alford

Kila Rose

Kimberly Shifflet

Kimo Forrest

KJ Ferguson

Krissy Feniak

Kristin Rambo

Kristy Lee

Kyle Bourgault

Kyle Wyley

Lacinda Thackeray

LakelIn Lemmings

Lance Curtis

Lance Wing

Lane Wyatt

Larissa

Larry Frick

Larry Gatlin

Larry Whitlock

Lathan Moore

Laura Lynn

Lauren Jolly

Lauren Riley

Leah Faith

Lee Gibson

Lee Newton

Libby Miller

Liquid Fire

Lisa Daggs

Lisa Daniel

Liz Moriondo

Lloyd Knight

Loretta Hooper

Lorrie Morgan

Lucas Hoge

Lucy Porter

Luis Rey

Madison Taylor Baez

Maggie Merrill

Magnolia Belle

Marcie Evans

Marie Kemph

Marie Norris

Mark209

Marquita Evans

Mary James

Mary Voorhies

Matt Chapel

Matt Gary

Megan Adams

Megan Arial

Meghan McGovern

Meghan Woods

Melissa Leigh

Melissa Wray

Mercy Shine

Michael Hall

Michael Salgado

Michael Salgado

Michael Sprinkle

Michelle Leigh

Mick Fury

Mikayla Lynn

Mariah Keefer

Misha Behner

Missy Hall

Molly Adele Brown

Morgan Dewey

Myranda Christi

Myron Parkinson

Nancy Childers

Neal McCoy

Nick Brennan

Nick Johnson

Nicole Silva

Niki Britt

Pam Tillis

Payton Williams

PJ Vann

Presley Smith

Preston Abraham

Priscilla Miller

Raven Davis

Ray Whitlock

Rebecca Lynn Howard

Regina Ballard

Rhonda Funk

Rhonda Vincent

Richard Noggin

Richard Schroder

Richie Fields

Rick Knowles

Ricky Crook

Ricky Thade Cole

Rob Carona

Robert Celluci

Robert Georg

Robert Stowell

Roger Dale

Running Wild Band

Ryan Goodwin

Ryan Price

Ryleigh Madison

Sam L Smith

Sara Avalos

Scott Brown

Seth Bunting

Shannon Grace

Shantell Ogden

Sharon Driscoll

Shawn Sackman

Shellem Cline

Simone De

Skye Moss

Skyliners

Soap Boxx

Sonja Stika

Sonny Thurnall

Sorena

Sol Brown

Susan Manion

Star Belle

Steve Bridgmon

Steven Cade

Stephanie Eisley

Stephanie Rabus

Stephen John

Simon

Stephen Rew

Stevie Lynn

Stronghold

Susan Walton

Suzzette Michaels

Tabitha Fair

Tammy Renee

Taylon Hope

T Graham Brown

TG Shephard

Ted Vigil

Tera Townsend

Tery Wayne

Theresa Fenger

Tia Hagg

Tim Gates

Timothy McGeary

Tim Rhodes

Tim Wright

Todd Stanford

Tommy Brandt

Tommy Brandt Jr.

Tommy Wesley

Tony Bridges

Tracy Lawrence

Trailer Trash Band

Trinity Wennerstrom

Troy Gonzalez

True Heart

Tyler Walker

Valerie Borman

Vince Gill

Wade Simms

Wes Whatley

Whitacre

Whitlocks

Will Haines

Will Hurd

William Shatner

Whitchita Worth

The Wait

Wyatt Laine

COMPANIES COREY IS AFFILIATED WITH

CCB Nashville

Corey Lee Publishing

Diamonds in The Rough Publishing

Emanant Music

Fame and Fortune Entertainment

Heartland Records

Imaginary Friends Music Partners

Inspirational Country Music Association

Ohana Music Group

March Family Music

MC1 Nashville Music Publishing

Molly Girl Music

Nashville Artist Development University

Norrisong Studios

Shay Watson Studios

Simply Grand Music

Songs of Hookline

Sweetsong Nashville

Ten7teen studios

Tennessee Songwriters Association International

The Josie Network Connection

Toe Tapper Music

World Fusion Music Productions

Don't miss Corey's other songwriting business books!

"The GPS for songwriters....a must read!" -*Patricia Dee Dee Smith, BMI, NextNumberOne Music Group, Target Top Ten Music & Pitchy Chicks Music*

"Read this book and turn your songs into a business…"
-*Barry Michael, CEO-Stockbrigde Records*

Printed by Amazon Italia Logistica S.r.l.
Torrazza Piemonte (TO), Italy